HOW TO EARN MORE MONEY

How to Earn More Money
Walter the Educator

Silent King Books
A WhichHead Entertainment Imprint

Copyright © 2024 by Walter the Educator

All rights reserved. No part of this book may be reproduced in any manner whatsoever without written permission except in the case of brief quotations embodied in critical articles and reviews.

First Printing, 2024

Disclaimer

The author and publisher offer this information without warranties expressed or implied. No matter the grounds, neither the author nor the publisher will be accountable for any losses, injuries, or other damages caused by the reader's use of this book. Your use of this book acknowledges an understanding and acceptance of this disclaimer.

How to Earn More Money is a little problem solver book by Walter the Educator that belongs to the Little Problem Solver Books Series. Collect them all and more books at WaltertheEducator.com

LITTLE PROBLEM SOLVER BOOKS

INTRO

In a world where financial independence has become an aspiration for many, learning How to Earn More Money is a critical skill that can significantly improve one's quality of life. Whether you are looking to supplement your existing income, start a new venture, or optimize your career, the pursuit of wealth involves strategy, discipline, and an understanding of the economic landscape. This little book explores various methods by which individuals can increase their income, from improving career prospects to exploring alternative sources of revenue. It covers both traditional approaches and modern innovations, offering practical tips that can be applied in different situations.

How to Earn More Money

1. Understanding the Basics of Income Growth

Before diving into specific strategies, it's important to understand the fundamental concepts behind earning money. Income generally comes from three main sources: wages or salary from employment, profits from business ventures, and passive income from investments. Each of these sources requires different levels of effort, risk, and skill.

How to Earn More Money

- **Active Income**: This is the money earned from work, such as wages, salaries, or profits from a small business. It is directly linked to the amount of time and effort you put in.

How to Earn More Money

- **Passive Income**: Passive income includes revenue streams that do not require constant effort. Examples include dividends from stocks, rental income from property, or royalties from creative work like books or music. Understanding the distinction between active and passive income helps frame the discussion on How to Earn More Money. Both can contribute to financial growth, and many successful individuals rely on a combination of the two.

How to Earn More Money

2. Enhancing Career Prospects

One of the most direct and reliable ways to increase your income is by advancing in your career. This requires a thoughtful approach that focuses on skill development, networking, and strategically positioning yourself for higher-paying opportunities.

How to Earn More Money

2.1 Education and Skills Development

One of the key drivers of higher earning potential is education. Higher levels of education tend to correlate with increased earning power, as more specialized skills often command higher salaries. Pursuing certifications, advanced degrees, or acquiring skills relevant to your field can set you apart in the job market.

How to Earn More Money

- **Identify In-Demand Skills**: Research the job market to determine which skills are in high demand. Fields like technology, healthcare, engineering, and data science often offer high-paying opportunities. Learning coding, project management, or financial analysis, for example, can significantly boost your earning potential.

How to Earn More Money

- **Continuing Education**: Even after securing a job, consider taking courses or attending workshops to stay updated with industry trends. Many employers offer tuition reimbursement for employees seeking to improve their skills.

How to Earn More Money

2.2 Networking and Building Professional Relationships

Networking is a powerful tool for career advancement. Building strong relationships within your industry can lead to job opportunities, partnerships, or mentorships that can accelerate your career.

How to Earn More Money

- **Join Professional Organizations**: Many industries have associations or groups where professionals can meet, share ideas, and create opportunities for collaboration. Being an active member of such organizations can help you stay visible to key decision-makers.

How to Earn More Money

- **Leverage Social Media**: Platforms like LinkedIn are essential for networking in today's professional landscape. Engage with industry leaders, share your expertise, and showcase your achievements to position yourself as a thought leader in your field.

How to Earn More Money

2.3 Negotiating for Higher Pay

If you are currently employed, one of the most straightforward ways to increase your income is by negotiating for a higher salary. Research shows that many people leave money on the table simply by failing to ask for a raise.

How to Earn More Money

- **Prepare Your Case**: Before entering into salary negotiations, make sure to document your achievements, showing how you've added value to the organization. Use this evidence to support your request for higher compensation.

How to Earn More Money

- **Market Research**: Investigate what others in your position, with similar experience, are earning. Websites like Glassdoor and PayScale can provide salary data for comparable jobs in your area.

How to Earn More Money

3. Starting a Side Hustle

In recent years, the concept of a "side hustle" has gained popularity as a way for people to increase their income outside of their full-time jobs. A side hustle can take many forms, from freelancing to selling products online. It offers flexibility and the potential for significant financial rewards.

How to Earn More Money

3.1 Freelancing and Consulting

Freelancing allows you to offer your skills and services on a contractual basis. It is a flexible option that lets you control your workload and pricing. Common freelancing fields include graphic design, writing, programming, and marketing.

How to Earn More Money

- **Use Online Platforms**: Websites like Upwork, Fiverr, and Freelancer provide a platform to connect with clients. Building a strong portfolio and gathering client reviews can help you secure higher-paying contracts over time.

How to Earn More Money

- **Consulting**: If you have significant expertise in a particular industry, consulting can be a lucrative side hustle. Companies are often willing to pay for expert advice to solve specific business problems. Consulting can be done on your own terms and is a great way to leverage your knowledge for financial gain.

How to Earn More Money

3.2 Monetizing a Hobby

Turning a passion or hobby into a side income is another popular route. For example, if you enjoy photography, you can sell prints or offer your services at events. If you like crafting, you can sell handmade items on platforms like Etsy.

How to Earn More Money

- **Create an Online Store**: E-commerce platforms like Shopify and Etsy make it easy to sell products online. Digital goods, like printables or courses, are especially attractive because they don't require physical inventory.

How to Earn More Money

- **Content Creation**: If you enjoy creating videos, writing blogs, or producing podcasts, you can earn money through advertising, sponsorships, or affiliate marketing. Platforms like YouTube, Twitch, and Patreon offer various monetization options for creators.

How to Earn More Money

4. Investing for Passive Income

Investing is one of the most powerful ways to grow wealth over time. By putting your money to work, you can create streams of passive income that continue to generate revenue even when you're not actively working.

How to Earn More Money

4.1 Stock Market Investments

The stock market is one of the most accessible ways to start investing. It offers the potential for substantial returns, especially when approached with a long-term mindset.

How to Earn More Money

- **Dividend Stocks**: Some companies pay dividends to shareholders, which can provide a regular income stream. Dividend-paying stocks are particularly attractive for those seeking passive income.

How to Earn More Money

- **Index Funds and ETFs**: For those new to investing, index funds and exchange-traded funds (ETFs) are low-cost options that provide diversification. They spread your investment across a variety of assets, reducing risk.

How to Earn More Money

4.2 Real Estate Investing

Real estate can be a highly profitable way to earn passive income, but it requires more capital upfront compared to other forms of investment.

How to Earn More Money

- **Rental Properties**: Buying properties to rent out is one of the most common forms of real estate investment. It provides a steady income stream, though managing rental properties can require time and effort.

How to Earn More Money

- **Real Estate Investment Trusts (REITs)**: For those who want exposure to real estate without the hassle of property management, REITs are an option. These are companies that own, operate, or finance income-producing real estate and pay dividends to shareholders.

How to Earn More Money

4.3 Peer-to-Peer Lending and Crowdfunding

Peer-to-peer (P2P) lending platforms allow you to lend money to individuals or small businesses in exchange for interest payments. Similarly, crowdfunding platforms enable you to invest in startups or real estate projects.

How to Earn More Money

- **Prosper and LendingClub**: These platforms offer opportunities to earn interest on loans. However, be mindful of the risks involved, as borrowers may default on payments.

How to Earn More Money

- **Equity Crowdfunding**: Platforms like SeedInvest or Republic allow you to invest in early-stage startups in exchange for equity. While risky, successful startups can offer substantial returns.

How to Earn More Money

5. Entrepreneurship and Starting a Business

Starting your own business offers the potential for unlimited income, but it also comes with risks and challenges. Entrepreneurs must be prepared to face uncertainty and put in significant effort to see their business succeed.

How to Earn More Money

5.1 Identifying a Profitable Niche

The first step in starting a business is identifying a profitable niche. Successful businesses often solve a specific problem or fulfill a need in the market.

How to Earn More Money

- **Market Research**: Conducting thorough market research is essential to understanding the competition, target audience, and demand for your product or service. This research will guide your business strategy and help you avoid costly mistakes.

How to Earn More Money

- **Unique Selling Proposition (USP)**: Your USP is what sets your business apart from competitors. It could be a lower price, better quality, or exceptional customer service. Clearly defining your USP can help attract customers and generate revenue.

How to Earn More Money

5.2 Scaling Your Business

Once your business is up and running, scaling it is key to increasing profits. This involves expanding operations, increasing customer acquisition, and optimizing processes.

How to Earn More Money

- **Automation and Outsourcing**: Streamlining your business operations by automating tasks or outsourcing can free up time and allow you to focus on growth. For example, using customer relationship management (CRM) software can automate marketing tasks, while outsourcing administrative duties can reduce your workload.

How to Earn More Money

- **Expanding Product Lines**: Offering new products or services can help you tap into new markets and increase your revenue. Diversification reduces reliance on a single revenue stream and can make your business more resilient.

How to Earn More Money

6. Cutting Expenses and Financial Discipline

While earning more money is important, managing your finances wisely is equally critical. Many individuals fail to achieve financial independence because they do not control their spending.

How to Earn More Money

6.1 Budgeting and Saving

A well-structured budget is the foundation of financial discipline. By tracking your income and expenses, you can identify areas where you can cut costs and increase savings.

How to Earn More Money

- **The 50/30/20 Rule**: A popular budgeting method is the 50/30/20 rule, where 50% of your income goes toward necessities, 30% toward discretionary spending, and 20% toward savings and investments.

How to Earn More Money

- **Emergency Fund**: Building an emergency fund is essential to protect yourself from unforeseen financial challenges, such as medical bills or job loss. A good rule of thumb is to save three to six months' worth of living expenses.

How to Earn More Money

6.2 Minimizing Debt

Debt can hinder your ability to accumulate wealth, especially high-interest debt like credit card balances. Prioritize paying off debt to free up more money for saving and investing.

How to Earn More Money

- **Debt Avalanche Method**: This approach involves paying off high-interest debts first while making minimum payments on other balances. This minimizes the amount of interest paid over time.

How to Earn More Money

- **Debt Snowball Method**: The debt snowball method focuses on paying off the smallest debts first to build momentum. While it may not minimize interest, it can be psychologically motivating.

How to Earn More Money

OUTRO

Earning more money requires a multifaceted approach that combines skill development, strategic investments, entrepreneurship, and financial discipline. Whether you choose to advance in your career, start a side hustle, or invest in long-term income streams, the key to financial growth is taking proactive steps toward your goals. Success in increasing your income doesn't happen overnight, but with persistence, knowledge, and the right strategies, anyone can achieve greater financial prosperity.

ABOUT THE CREATOR

Walter the Educator is one of the pseudonyms for Walter Anderson. Formally educated in Chemistry, Business, and Education, he is an educator, an author, a diverse entrepreneur, and he is the son of a disabled war veteran. "Walter the Educator" shares his time between educating and creating. He holds interests and owns several creative projects that entertain, enlighten, enhance, and educate, hoping to inspire and motivate you. Follow, find new works, and stay up to date with Walter the Educator™ at WaltertheEducator.com

www.ingramcontent.com/pod-product-compliance
Lightning Source LLC
LaVergne TN
LVHW012038060526
838201LV00061B/4667

EDUCATION | SELF-HELP

How to Earn More Money is a little problem solver book by Walter the Educator that belongs to the Little Problem Solver Books Series. Collect them all and more books at WaltertheEducator.com

SKB
Silent King Books

काव्य

मेरे अल्फ़ाज़.....

तनिश जैन